MW00984375

How to Cook for Your Man

Still Want to Look at Him Naked

Oxmoor House®

HOW TO COOK FOR YOUR MAN

&

Still Want to Look at Him
NAKED

By Lori and Vicki Todd

Published 1996 by Oxmoor House, Inc.
Book Division of Southern Progress Corporation

©1996 by Lori Todd and Vicki Todd Roos

Library of Congress Catalog Card Number: 96-69490
ISBN: 0-8487-1551-9
Manufactured in the United States of America
First Printing 1996

Editor-in-Chief: Nancy Fitzpatrick Wyatt
Senior Foods Editor: Susan Carlisle Payne
Senior Editor, Editorial Services: Olivia Kindig Wells
Art Director: James Boone

How to Cook for Your Man & Still Want to Look at Him Naked

Foods Editor: Janice Krahn Hanby
Copy Editor: Keri Bradford Anderson
Editorial Assistant: Alison Rich Lewis
Production Designer: Eleanor Cameron
Production and Distribution Director: Phillip Lee
Associate Production Manager: Vanessa Cobbs Richardson
Production Assistant: Valerie L. Heard

Cover and Interior Photography by Michael St. John

To order more copies of
**How to Cook for Your Man &
Still Want to Look at Him Naked,**
write to:
Oxmoor House
P.O. Box 2463, Birmingham, AL 35201

Thanks to You

This book is dedicated to our parents, John and
Bev Todd, and to Vicki's husband, Bradley Roos. Mom always
encouraged us to experiment in the kitchen and to pursue our
passions. Dad taught us to persevere because good things come
to those who wait. Bradley was our guinea pig and helped us
test all the recipes for "real man appeal."

Lori Todd   *Vicki Todd*

What's in It for You

Behind Every Great Man . . .

Americans get heavier every year, and chances are that your Honey is one of them. Instead of smirking, help him keep his weight in check. Not only will this reduce his risk of heart disease, diabetes, and cancer, but it will also reduce his pot belly!

This book was developed for all of the women in this world who have tried to help their men lose weight and then found resistance. All men have their favorite foods, which typically don't include "diet" food. To help with their metamorphoses, we created recipes that will slim them down *and* make meals satisfying for the two of you.

Until now, you have been inundated with quick weight loss solutions and new health fads. The fact is, they don't work. Our philosophy is simple—everything in moderation!

Limit fat, calories, and alcohol; eat three meals a day; exercise; and don't smoke. If you must eat "fast food," figure out your best alternatives, and limit the amount you order. Turn to the grocery store deli for shortcut opportunities like pre-washed vegetables and salads, rotisserie chicken, and low-fat side dishes. Read food labels, watch portion sizes, and move, move, move! Take the stairs, go for a walk, play tennis, or fool around together.

Onward, Ladies! Preserve our dream. Let every man in our divine presence possess a washboard stomach and, of course, a fat wallet!

Intimate Details

There are a few things you should know when using our recipes.

- **Every recipe has less than 30% of calories from fat.** We've decided, however, not to include nutritional analyses because we want you to have **fun**, not be a slave to numbers. Be assured that we've figured everything out for you behind closed doors. Relax and enjoy!

- **Our portion sizes are realistic.** He won't go away from the table hungry. Many of our recipes are for more than two people, so if you're cooking for only two, freeze the leftovers—don't let him eat them.

- **We use potatoes in a lot of our recipes.** That's because men love potatoes. They're satisfying, nutritious, and easy to prepare; yet they're low in fat and calories. Best of all, men are clueless to these facts and believe that potatoes are the foundation of a Mighty Man's meal.

- **We like to use egg substitutes when appropriate.** They taste better than using just egg whites and are as good as whole eggs.

- **We use vegetable cooking spray in almost every recipe.** It's our foundation for sautéing ingredients and for coating cookwear. Vegetable cooking spray also comes in olive oil and butter flavors. It has only 7 calories and less than 1 gram of fat per serving—a skinny comparison to the 13 grams of fat and 122 calories in 1 tablespoon of vegetable oil.

- **Here are some final woman-to-woman cooking tips:**

1. <u>Shhhhh—Don't Tell Him.</u> Don't tell him that the meal you're making is low in fat. Never use the words, "It's good for you." When men hear those words, they instantly make up their minds that the light dish won't be tasty.

2. <u>Bait and Switch.</u> If his taste buds have grown accustomed to products like real mayonnaise, salad dressing, sour cream, whole milk, and butter, convert him slowly. First, reel him in with a combination of the real product and its low-fat version. Gradually, switch entirely to the low-fat product and eventually to the nonfat one. Peel off the labels if you have to, so he won't know what you're cooking with. Tell him you needed the label because there is a recipe on the back.

continued

3. <u>The Eye Doesn't Lie.</u> Serve entrées with a vegetable and a salad. He'll think you've make a big, well-rounded meal, and he'll be full without getting fat.

4. <u>It's All in the Hand.</u> Portion size that is. Most people underestimate the amount of food they eat. A serving size for meat, poultry, and fish is about the size of your palm, minus the fingers. A serving size of pasta, cereal, vegetables, and milk is the size of your fist. A portion of cheese is the size of the very tip (last digit) of your index finger.

Remember, go about these lifestyle changes slowly and quietly. The turtle always beats the hare. Soon your man will be in fighting shape, and so will you. You'll both feel healthier and more energetic. Get off the couch and into each other's arms!

Skinny Dip
Roasted Pepper and Garlic Dip

Garlic is amazing. It can lower blood pressure, decrease bad cholesterol, and increase good cholesterol. Garlic may even prevent cancer. With this dip, you're taking care of your man's health, as well as his appetite.

3   cloves garlic, unpeeled
1   large red bell pepper, roasted (see facing page) or 1 (12-ounce) jar roasted red peppers, drained and patted dry

1   cup nonfat cream cheese, softened
2   teaspoons balsamic vinegar
¼   teaspoon ground red pepper

Place garlic on a piece of aluminum foil. Broil 5½ inches from heat 3 minutes on each side or until charred. Let cool; remove skin. Position knife blade in food processor bowl; add garlic pulp and roasted pepper. Process until smooth. Add cream cheese, vinegar, and ground red pepper; process until blended. Cover and chill at least 1 hour before serving. Serve with low-fat crackers or raw vegetables. Yield: 1⅓ cups.

MOTHER NEVER TOLD YOU

Here's the skinny on roasting garlic and bell peppers:
To roast a head of garlic, *peel off most of the papery outer layer of skin. Cut off top one-third of garlic head. Wrap garlic in a piece of aluminum foil, and bake at 500° for 30 minutes. Squeeze the garlic cloves to extract the pulp, and discard the skin.* ***To roast bell peppers***, *cut them in half lengthwise; remove and discard seeds and membranes. Place peppers, skin side up, on a baking sheet, and flatten with palm of hand. Broil 5½ inches from heat 15 to 20 minutes or until charred. Place peppers in ice water until cool. Peel and discard skins.*

He'll Get Hot Under the Collar
Stuffed Jalapeños

Experts say that capsaicin, the fiery component of jalapeño peppers, is an aphrodisiac. Serve your sweetie these stuffed peppers, and be prepared to reap the benefits!

12   large fresh jalapeño peppers
½   cup nonfat cream cheese, softened
¼   cup (1 ounce) shredded reduced-fat
      mozzarella cheese

¼   cup grated Parmesan cheese
     Vegetable cooking spray
     Salsa

Cut peppers in half lengthwise; remove seeds. Combine cheeses; spoon evenly into pepper halves. Place in a 13- x 9- x 2-inch baking dish coated with cooking spray. Bake, uncovered, at 350° for 30 minutes or until bubbly and lightly browned. Serve warm with salsa. Yield: 6 appetizer servings.

Lip-Smackin' Cheese Tease
Chile Relleno Cheese Bars

Serve this decadent appetizer to the one you love, and don't worry about his waistline—a cheese bar weighs in at a mere 1.5 grams of fat.

1   cup egg substitute
1   cup nonfat cottage cheese
¼   cup all-purpose flour
½   teaspoon baking powder
1   (4.5-ounce) can chopped green
     chiles, drained
½   teaspoon hot sauce

⅓   cup (1.3 ounces) shredded reduced-fat sharp Cheddar cheese
⅓   cup (1.3 ounces) shredded reduced-fat mozzarella cheese
     Vegetable cooking spray
     Salsa

Beat egg substitute in a mixing bowl at medium speed of an electric mixer 1 minute. Gradually add cottage cheese, flour, and baking powder, beating until smooth. Stir in chiles and next 3 ingredients. Pour into an 8-inch square pan coated with cooking spray. Bake, uncovered, at 400° for 15 minutes; reduce heat to 350°, and bake 35 additional minutes or until firm. Let stand 15 minutes. Cut into 12 bars. Serve warm with salsa. Yield: 6 appetizer servings.

Mi Casa, Su Casa Quesadilla
Shrimp and Cilantro Quesadilla

To help slim down your Muchacho, top these appetizer quesadillas with salsa instead of fat-laden guacamole and sour cream. Try them as an entrée snuggled up to fat-free black beans or refried beans.

7	unpeeled medium-size fresh shrimp	2	(8-inch) fat-free flour tortillas
½	cup water	¼	cup (1 ounce) shredded reduced-fat Cheddar cheese
1	clove garlic, chopped	¼	cup (1 ounce) shredded reduced-fat mozzarella cheese
1	green bell pepper, diced	¼	cup seeded, chopped tomato
1	tablespoon chopped fresh cilantro or 1 teaspoon dried cilantro		Salsa (optional)
⅛	teaspoon ground red pepper		Nonfat sour cream (optional)
⅛	teaspoon chili powder		Chopped fresh cilantro (optional)
	Vegetable cooking spray		

Peel shrimp, and devein, if desired. Chop shrimp; set aside.

Combine water and garlic in a large nonstick skillet; cover and cook over medium heat 5 minutes. Add shrimp and green bell pepper, and cook 3 to 5 minutes or until shrimp turn pink, stirring often. Remove from heat; drain. Place shrimp mixture in bowl; add 1 tablespoon cilantro, ground red pepper, and chili powder, and toss gently. Set aside.

Coat a large nonstick skillet with cooking spray, and place over medium-low heat until hot. Spray 1 side of a tortilla with cooking spray; place tortilla, sprayed side down, in skillet. Top with shrimp mixture; sprinkle with cheeses and tomato. Top with remaining tortilla, and spray with cooking spray. Cover and cook 5 minutes; turn and cook 5 additional minutes. Cut into wedges. If desired, top with salsa, sour cream, and additional cilantro. Yield: 4 appetizer servings.

Things
MOTHER NEVER TOLD YOU

Though commonly thought of as a vegetable, a tomato is actually a fruit. Once thought to have aphrodisiacal powers, tomatoes have been called pommes d'amour, or "love apples" by the French. A fresh medium-size tomato is virtually fat-free and has only about 25 calories. Tomatoes are also an excellent source of vitamin C.

Love at First Bite Strudel

Crab, Pear, and Brie Strudel

If you're having your Honey's boss or his family over for dinner, impress them with this appetizer. Or serve it as the entrée when you're having a more intimate gathering.

  6   ounces Brie
  ½   pound fresh lump crabmeat,
        drained
2½   cups peeled, chopped fresh pears
  ¼   cup finely chopped green onions
  ⅛   teaspoon grated lemon rind
  2   teaspoons fresh lemon juice

  ¼   teaspoon ground white pepper
  1   clove garlic, minced
  7   sheets frozen phyllo pastry,
        thawed
        Butter-flavored vegetable cooking
        spray

Remove and discard rind from Brie. Cut Brie into ½-inch cubes. Combine Brie, crabmeat, and next 6 ingredients in a large bowl, stirring gently.

Place 1 sheet of phyllo on a flat surface (keep remaining phyllo covered with a slightly damp towel). Lightly spray phyllo with cooking spray. Layer remaining sheets of phyllo on top of first sheet, spraying each with cooking spray.

Spoon crabmeat mixture along a short side of phyllo, leaving a 3-inch edge; fold edge over crabmeat mixture. Fold both long edges of phyllo in 2 inches. Start at filled short side, and roll phyllo, jellyroll fashion, keeping long edges tucked while rolling. Place strudel, seam side down, on a baking sheet coated with cooking spray. Score diamond shapes in top of strudel with a sharp knife. Lightly spray strudel with cooking spray. Bake, uncovered, at 375° for 30 minutes or until golden. Let stand 5 minutes before serving. Yield: 6 appetizer or 3 entrée servings.

He's No Loafer
Lamb Loaf

Men love satisfying appetizers, so give them what they want. This hearty, make-ahead appetizer is perfect for a romantic picnic. Serve slices of the loaf on a crisp flat bread or French bread (both are low in fat) spread with mustard. Don't forget to pack a nice bottle of Chardonnay to toast to l'amour!

Vegetable cooking spray
4 cups finely chopped fresh mushrooms (about 1 pound)
¾ cup finely chopped onion
2 cloves garlic, minced
⅓ cup dry white wine
½ cup egg substitute
2 teaspoons dried thyme
1 teaspoon salt
1 teaspoon dried rosemary
½ teaspoon ground white pepper
¼ teaspoon ground red pepper
2 pounds extra-lean ground lamb
1 cup quick-cooking oats, uncooked
¼ cup chopped fresh parsley or 1½ tablespoons dried parsley flakes
3 tablespoons dried mint flakes

Coat a large nonstick skillet with cooking spray; place over medium heat until hot. Add mushrooms, onion, and garlic, and cook, stirring constantly, until tender.

Add wine, and cook over medium-high heat 5 minutes, stirring often. Remove from heat, and set aside.

Combine egg substitute and next 5 ingredients in a large bowl, stirring well. Add lamb, oats, parsley, and mint; stir well. Stir in mushroom mixture. Shape mixture into a 9- x 5- x 3-inch loaf. Place loaf on a rack coated with cooking spray; place in a shallow roasting pan. Bake, uncovered, at 350° for 1 hour and 15 minutes. Remove from oven, and let stand 20 minutes. Cover and chill at least 8 hours before serving to allow flavors to blend. Yield: 16 appetizer servings.

Buenas Noches Beverage
Margarita

Loosen him up by serving a Margarita before dinner. There's no sugar in this recipe, because the original Margarita contained none. This recipe is the best we've ever tasted.

Lime wedge
Margarita salt
Crushed ice
2 parts fresh lime juice

2 parts Triple Sec or other orange-flavored liqueur
1 part tequila

Rub rim of a glass with lime wedge. Place salt in a saucer; spin rim of glass in salt. Fill glass with crushed ice. Combine lime juice, Triple Sec, and tequila; stir well. Pour over ice. Yield: 1 serving.

Getting in
the Mood
Salads & Soups

Seize-the-Moment Salad
Caesar Salad

The traditional fat-laden Caesar salad is a sure way to kiss his healthy diet good-bye. Our version is filled with flavor, not fat. Plus, it's a great opportunity to use our "Bait and Switch" technique (see page 9). If your dream man isn't accustomed to the taste of nonfat mayonnaise, try substituting the reduced-fat version. Then gradually switch to nonfat mayonnaise. Eventually, you'll wonder why you ever ate regular mayonnaise, with over 175 grams of fat per cup, in the first place.

⅔ cup nonfat mayonnaise
⅓ cup lemon juice
¼ cup grated Parmesan cheese
1 tablespoon anchovy paste

2 cloves garlic, minced
1 head romaine lettuce, torn into bite-sized pieces
16 croutons (see facing page)

Combine first 5 ingredients in a small bowl, and stir well. Cover dressing, and chill at least 1 hour.

To serve, toss lettuce with chilled dressing. Sprinkle salad with croutons. Yield: 4 servings.

Homemade croutons add great crunch and flavor to a salad without adding much fat, and they're easy to make. Simply cut day-old French bread into cubes, and place on a baking sheet. Spray all sides of cubes with olive oil-flavored vegetable cooking spray. Sprinkle with garlic salt and pepper to taste. Bake at 400° for 8 to 10 minutes or until crisp and lightly browned. Let cool. Store any leftover croutons in an airtight container.

Make Him Tenderhearted
Hearts of Palm Salad

A good salad counts toward the recommended 3 to 5 servings of vegetables per day. Keep cans of hearts of palm on hand to make this snappy little salad any time you please, and you'll never be brokenhearted.

1	head radicchio, separated into leaves	½	cup balsamic vinegar
1	(14¼-ounce) can hearts of palm	1	ounce feta cheese, crumbled
4	Roma tomatoes, sliced	1½	teaspoons dried basil

Arrange radicchio leaves on individual salad plates. Rinse hearts of palm under cool water; drain and slice. Arrange hearts of palm and tomato slices on top of radicchio leaves. Drizzle vinegar over salads. Top each salad evenly with feta cheese and basil. Yield: 4 servings.

If you really want to schmooze the one you love, serve the dressing for a salad in a Roma tomato. Just cut 1/4 inch off the top of tomato, and set top aside. Scoop out the seeds and membranes with a spoon, and fill tomato with dressing. Replace the tomato top. For extra oomph, serve the salad on chilled plates with chilled forks.

Olive Oil's Secret
Warm Spinach Salad

Salad dressing is one of the main sources of fat in a man's diet. Pump up your man's physique by serving him this muscle-building salad topped with a healthy "un"dressing.

1 large bunch fresh spinach
2 hard-cooked eggs, sliced
1 red onion, thinly sliced
½ cup nonfat mayonnaise
¼ cup sugar

¼ cup red wine vinegar
16 croutons (see page 25)
2 slices turkey bacon, cooked and crumbled

Arrange spinach, egg slices, and onion evenly on individual salad plates. Combine mayonnaise, sugar, and vinegar in a small saucepan. Cook over low heat, stirring constantly with a wire whisk, until smooth. Spoon warm dressing evenly over salads. Top with croutons and bacon. Serve immediately. Yield: 4 servings.

Spice-It-Up Slaw
Pineapple 'n' Jalapeño Coleslaw

Researchers have found that some deli-prepared coleslaws contain as much as 85% more calories than the delicatessen nutritional summaries state. Make your own slaw, and you'll know exactly what you're putting into his beautiful body.

1 cup nonfat mayonnaise
1 cup nonfat sour cream
3 tablespoons sugar
3 tablespoons Dijon mustard
2 tablespoons lemon juice
¼ teaspoon salt
½ medium green cabbage, shredded (about 4 cups)

½ medium-size red cabbage, shredded (about 4 cups)
1 (15¼-ounce) can pineapple chunks, drained
5 pickled jalapeño peppers, finely chopped
3 green onions, sliced

Combine first 6 ingredients in a small bowl; stir well. Combine cabbages, pineapple, and pepper in a large bowl. Add mayonnaise mixture, and toss gently. Sprinkle with green onions. Serve immediately. Yield: 8 servings.

Stud Spud Special
Classic Potato Salad

Mom has been making this classic potato salad for Dad for over 40 years. She started making it the "skinny" way about 5 years ago, and Dad never caught on. She reduced the fat by using nonfat mayonnaise-type salad dressing and fewer hard-cooked egg yolks. Each egg yolk contains 63 calories and 5.9 grams of fat. Remember this fact every time you use egg yolks, and the "yolk" will never be on you!

5 medium-size red potatoes, peeled and cut into 1-inch cubes	2 tablespoons sweet pickle juice
½ cup chopped sweet pickles	1½ tablespoons skim milk
¼ cup finely chopped onion	1 tablespoon red wine vinegar
5 hard-cooked egg whites, chopped	1½ teaspoons salt
2 hard-cooked egg yolks, chopped	¼ teaspoon sugar
¼ cup nonfat mayonnaise-type salad dressing	⅛ teaspoon dry mustard
	⅛ teaspoon ground red pepper
	Paprika

Cook potato cubes in boiling water to cover 10 minutes (do not overcook; potato cubes should be firm). Drain well.

Place potato cubes in large bowl. Add sweet pickle, onion, egg whites, and egg yolks; toss gently.

Combine salad dressing and next 7 ingredients in a small bowl; stir well. Add dressing mixture to potato mixture, and toss gently. Cover and chill. Sprinkle with paprika just before serving. Yield: 6 servings.

Things
MOTHER NEVER TOLD YOU

Hard cooking eggs is simple. Just place the desired number of eggs in a single layer in a saucepan. Then add enough water to measure at least 1 inch over the eggs. Cover and bring just to a boil. Remove the pan from the heat, and let stand, covered, in hot water, 15 to 17 minutes for large eggs. Pour off the water, and immediately run cold water over the eggs until they are cool enough to handle.

He'll Long to Go South of the Border
Mexican Salad

Almost everyone craves a taco salad now and then, but a typical restaurant version contains a whopping 650 calories and 47 grams of fat per serving. Ours is made with extra-lean ground sirloin; buying it can be a good technique for meeting a man. If you're single, and the butcher is cute, ask him to grind it fresh for you.

4   (10-inch) fat-free flour tortillas
Vegetable cooking spray
1   pound extra-lean ground sirloin
1   (¼-ounce) envelope taco seasoning mix
1   (8-ounce) can whole kernel corn, drained
1   (4.5-ounce) can chopped green chiles, drained

½   (16-ounce) can fat-free refried beans
1   head iceberg lettuce, torn
½   cup chopped onion
1   cup (4 ounces) shredded reduced-fat Cheddar cheese
1   tomato, seeded and chopped
Salsa (optional)
Chopped fresh cilantro (optional)
Sliced jalapeño peppers (optional)

To make tortilla shells, roll 4 pieces of aluminum foil into balls about the size of an orange. Spray both sides of tortillas with cooking spray, and place over balls to form upside-down bowls. Place bowls, tortilla sides up, on a baking sheet. Bake at 350° for 10 minutes or until crisp. Remove foil; let tortilla shells cool.

Cook ground sirloin in a nonstick skillet over medium heat until browned, stirring until it crumbles; drain well. Add taco seasoning mix according to package directions; set aside. Combine corn and chiles in a small bowl; stir well. Meanwhile, heat refried beans according to can directions.

To assemble salad, layer the following evenly in each tortilla shell: lettuce, sirloin, beans, corn mixture, onion, cheese, tomato, and, if desired, optional ingredients. Serve immediately. Yield: 4 servings.

Things
MOTHER NEVER TOLD YOU

You can remove much of the fat from ground meats after browning by rinsing the crumbled meat in a strainer under running water. You'll know that the fat has been removed when the water runs clear.

He-Won't-Become-Chicken-Fat Salad
Chicken, Apple, and Raisin Salad

If you're tired of high-fat chicken salad with little flavor, look no further. The blue cheese dressing in our salad packs a flavorful punch!

1 (8-ounce) carton plain nonfat
   yogurt
1 apple, unpeeled, cored, and
   chopped
2 tablespoons lemon juice
1 head romaine or Bibb lettuce, torn
   (about 3 cups)

1 cup cooked, chopped chicken breast
1 cup diced celery (about 2 stalks)
½ cup golden raisins
1 tablespoon slivered almonds, toasted
¾ cup nonfat buttermilk
1 teaspoon cider vinegar
3 ounces blue cheese, crumbled

Spread yogurt to 1-inch thickness on top of several layers of paper towels. Cover with additional towels. Let stand 5 minutes. Scrape yogurt into a bowl. Set aside.

Combine apple and lemon juice in a large bowl; toss gently. Add lettuce and next 4 ingredients; toss gently. Set aside.

Combine reserved yogurt, buttermilk, and vinegar in a small bowl; stir in cheese. Add to chicken mixture, and toss gently. Serve immediately. Yield: 4 servings.

Drive-Him-Wild Rice Salad
Wild Rice-Seafood Salad

Is your Romeo too busy to stop for lunch? Make this hearty salad for supper, and you'll have enough left over to pack for his meal the next day.

4 cups Chicken Stock (see page 40) or canned fat-free chicken broth
1 cup wild rice, uncooked
1½ pounds fresh crabmeat, drained and flaked
1 pound unpeeled medium-size fresh shrimp, cooked, peeled, and deveined
1½ cups frozen English peas, thawed

1 cup diced celery (about 2 stalks)
½ cup chopped green onions
1 cup nonfat mayonnaise
1 cup nonfat sour cream
⅓ cup orange juice
1 tablespoon curry powder
2 tablespoons chutney
2 cloves garlic, minced
1 bunch curly endive, torn

Combine Chicken Stock and rice in a saucepan; bring to a boil. Cover, reduce heat, and simmer 1 hour or until tender. Drain, if necessary. Combine rice, crabmeat, and next 4 ingredients in a large bowl. Combine mayonnaise and next 5 ingredients; add to rice mixture, and toss. Cover and chill. Serve on endive. Yield: 8 servings.

King of the Sea
Curried Tuna Salad

Make this tuna for your big kahuna to help ensure that he'll have a long and healthy life. Tuna is rich in omega-3 fatty acids, which have been shown to help prevent heart disease. Plus, the parsley contains a substance that reduces the accumulation of plaque on artery walls and protects against cancer.

¾ cup nonfat mayonnaise	1 cup peeled, finely chopped apple
½ cup plain nonfat yogurt	½ cup raisins, plumped
2 tablespoons curry powder	¼ cup cashews, toasted and chopped
2 tablespoons lemon juice	¼ cup chopped sweet pickles
1 pound fresh tuna, cooked and flaked or 2 (12-ounce) cans tuna in water, drained and flaked	3 tablespoons minced green onions
	1 head romaine lettuce, torn
	¼ cup chopped fresh parsley

Combine first 4 ingredients; stir well. Combine tuna and next 5 ingredients in a large bowl; toss gently. Add mayonnaise mixture, and toss gently. Cover and chill 1 hour. Toss lettuce and parsley; spoon tuna salad over lettuce mixture on individual salad plates. Yield: 4 servings.

Our Men Like It Hot
Potato-Leek Soup

The French serve potato soup chilled and call it "vichyssoise." We find that hot-blooded American men like it served warm. It's perfect for a cold winter's evening. Make sure to build a nice fire, inside and outside the fireplace!

6	cups Chicken Stock (see page 40) or canned fat-free chicken broth	4	cups peeled, diced baking potatoes
4	cups sliced leeks (the white part and a bit of the green stem)	⅛	teaspoon salt
		⅛	teaspoon ground white pepper
		½	cup nonfat sour cream

Combine first 3 ingredients in a stockpot; bring to a boil. Cover, reduce heat, and simmer 30 minutes or until potato is tender. Stir in salt and pepper.

To serve, ladle soup into individual soup bowls; top each serving with 1 table-spoon sour cream. Yield: 8 (1-cup) servings.

Note: For a creamy soup, simmer the vegetable mixture 40 minutes, and let cool 15 minutes. Transfer vegetable mixture in batches to container of an electric blender; cover and process until smooth. Return mixture to pan, and cook until thoroughly heated.

Ooh Là Là Soup
French Onion Soup with Vermouth

If your boy-toy is man enough, don a little French maid's costume to serve this soup. You'll be saying "Oui, Oui" all night long.

8	cups thinly sliced onions (about 2½ pounds)	2	tablespoons all-purpose flour
1	cup water	10	cups canned fat-free beef broth, divided
1	tablespoon olive oil	1	cup dry vermouth
½	teaspoon sugar	¼	cup brandy
½	teaspoon salt	8	cheesy croutons (see facing page)

Combine first 3 ingredients in a stockpot. Cover and cook over low heat, stirring constantly, 10 minutes or until translucent. Add sugar and salt; cook, uncovered, 25 to 30 minutes or until onions are lightly browned and caramelized, stirring often. (Add 2 tablespoons water to prevent sticking, if necessary.)

Combine flour and ¼ cup broth, stirring until smooth. Add to onion mixture, stirring until blended. Add remaining 9¾ cups broth, stirring with a wire whisk until blended. Add vermouth and brandy; simmer, uncovered, 2 hours, stirring occasionally.

To serve, ladle into individual soup bowls; top each serving with a crouton. Yield: 8 (1-cup) servings.

MOTHER NEVER TOLD YOU

It's easy to make large, crusty cheese croutons that are great for topping soup. Place eight slices of day-old French bread on a baking sheet coated with cooking spray. Spray both sides of the bread with cooking spray. Bake at 350° for 7 to 8 minutes or until lightly browned. Top each slice of bread with a slice of nonfat Swiss cheese. Return to the oven, and bake 5 additional minutes or until cheese melts. Très elegant!

Couple's Cure-All
Chicken Stock

Making your own chicken stock has many benefits. First, you'll have a rich-tasting stock you can use in countless recipes. Second, you can use the chicken meat in salads and sandwiches. Third, the pleasant aroma will fill your home, and your man will be impressed that you're making your own stock.

1	(3-pound) broiler-fryer with giblets	½	cup chopped onion
3	quarts water	2	teaspoons salt
3	stalks celery (including tops), cut into 1-inch pieces	5	or 6 black peppercorns
2	carrots, cut into 1-inch pieces	1	clove garlic
1	turnip, cut into 1-inch pieces	1	bay leaf

Place chicken and giblets in a large stockpot; add water. Add celery and remaining ingredients; bring to a boil. Cover, reduce heat, and simmer 2 hours, skimming fat and foam from surface as it rises to the top. Remove chicken; reserve for other uses. Pour stock through a strainer, discarding solids. Degrease stock. Store in refrigerator up to 3 days or in freezer up to 1 month. Yield: about 2 quarts.

Man Courses

Entrées

Body Buffer
Pork Loin with Apple-Raisin Stuffing

Your Tarzan will think that you're anything but a plain Jane when you serve him this elegant pork loin dish. The meat is stuffed with a light fruit mixture so that your man won't have to let out his loin cloth.

¼   cup finely chopped shallots
Vegetable cooking spray
1½ cups peeled, cored, and finely chopped apple
½   cup fine, dry breadcrumbs
½   cup finely chopped golden raisins
½   cup water
¼   cup finely chopped dried apricots
2   tablespoons chopped fresh parsley
¼   teaspoon salt

¼   teaspoon ground white pepper
1   (1½-pound) butterflied boneless pork loin, trimmed
1   teaspoon dried rosemary
1   teaspoon dried thyme
1   teaspoon dried oregano
¾   cup unsweetened apple juice
2   tablespoons brandy
1   tablespoon cornstarch
1   teaspoon sugar

Cook shallot in a small nonstick skillet coated with cooking spray over medium heat, stirring constantly, until tender. (Add 2 tablespoons water to prevent sticking, if necessary.) Combine shallot, apple, and next 7 ingredients in a large bowl; stir well. Spread apple mixture down center of pork loin, leaving a ½-inch border at sides. (If you have any leftover stuffing, place it in a small casserole, and bake at 350° for 20 minutes.) Roll up pork, jellyroll fashion, starting at short side. Secure at 2-inch intervals with cooking twine. Spray with cooking spray.

Combine rosemary, thyme, and oregano; rub over pork. Place pork, seam side down, on a rack coated with cooking spray. Place rack in a shallow roasting pan. Insert meat thermometer into thickest part of pork. Cover and bake at 350° for 1 hour and 25 minutes or until thermometer registers 160°. Let stand 10 minutes before serving.

While pork is standing, combine apple juice, brandy, cornstarch, and sugar in a small saucepan, whisking until blended. Bring to a boil; boil 1 minute, stirring constantly, until thickened. Serve sauce with pork. Yield: 4 servings.

MOTHER NEVER TOLD YOU

Your butcher will butterfly a pork loin for you. Call and let him know what you want before you go shopping, so the pork will be ready by the time you get there.

He's a Softie on the Inside
Herb-Crusted Pork Tenderloin

We like to serve this pork tenderloin with Olive Oil's Secret (see page 28) or with Savage Cabbage (see page 71). This tenderloin can be made ahead and either reheated or served chilled. This will give you and your honey more time to indulge in dessert before dinner.

½	cup nonfat mayonnaise		¼	teaspoon salt
¼	cup prepared mustard		¼	teaspoon pepper
1	tablespoon fennel seeds		1	(1-pound) pork tenderloin, trimmed
1	tablespoon dried rosemary			
1	tablespoon dried basil			Vegetable cooking spray

Combine mayonnaise and mustard in a small bowl; stir well. Stir in fennel seeds and next 4 ingredients. Coat pork thoroughly with mixture. Chill 1 hour. Place pork on a rack in a roasting pan coated with cooking spray. Bake at 375° for 30 minutes or until meat thermometer registers 160°. Let stand 5 minutes before serving. Yield: 4 servings.

Keep the Fire Burning
Chunky Red Chili

Your man will appreciate the chunks of sirloin steak in this chili.

1½ pounds sirloin steak, trimmed and cut into ½-inch cubes

4 (4.5-ounce) cans diced green chiles, drained

1 medium onion, chopped

1½ cups Chicken Stock (see page 40), divided

2 (15-ounce) cans red kidney beans, drained

1 (15-ounce) can tomato sauce

¼ cup paprika

2½ teaspoons ground cumin

2½ teaspoons chili powder

2 teaspoons ground oregano

1 teaspoon ground red pepper

¼ teaspoon salt

3 tablespoons masa flour

½ cup water

Combine steak, green chiles, onion, and ½ cup Chicken Stock in a stockpot; cook over medium heat 10 minutes. Add remaining 1 cup stock, beans, and next 7 ingredients; cover, reduce heat, and simmer 45 minutes. Combine masa flour and water, stirring to form a paste. Gradually add to chili, stirring constantly; simmer 10 additional minutes. Yield: 6 servings.

Let's Do a Hat Dance
Chiles Rellenos Casserole

Traditional Mexican cuisine is loaded with fat. When you crave the spicy fare, make this easy low-fat casserole.

1 cup chopped onion
2 cloves garlic, minced
¼ cup water
½ pound extra-lean ground beef, browned and rinsed (see page 33)
1½ teaspoons dried oregano
½ teaspoon ground cumin
¼ teaspoon salt
¼ teaspoon pepper
2 (4½-ounce) cans whole green chiles
Vegetable cooking spray

1 cup (4 ounces) shredded reduced-fat Cheddar cheese, divided
1 (16-ounce) can fat-free refried beans
1 (11-ounce) can whole kernel corn, drained
2 jalapeño peppers, seeded and sliced
⅓ cup all-purpose flour
1⅓ cups skim milk
½ teaspoon hot sauce
¼ teaspoon salt
1 cup egg substitute

Cook onion and garlic in water in a large nonstick skillet over medium heat 5 minutes. Add cooked ground beef, oregano, and next 3 ingredients.

46

Drain green chiles, and cut lengthwise into 4 pieces.

Arrange half of green chile strips in an 11- x 7- x 1½-inch baking dish coated with cooking spray. Top with ½ cup cheese. Spread beef mixture over cheese, leaving a ½-inch border around edges. Spread refried beans over beef mixture. Top with corn and peppers. Arrange remaining chile strips over corn; sprinkle with remaining ½ cup cheese.

Combine flour, milk, hot sauce, and ¼ teaspoon salt in a bowl, stirring with a wire whisk until blended. Whisk in egg substitute. Pour over mixture in dish. Bake, uncovered, at 350° for 1 hour and 10 minutes. Let stand 5 minutes before serving. Yield: 6 servings.

He'll Be True
Chicken Cordon Bleu

Set the scene for serving this dish with a bottle of oil and a deep-fat fryer on the counter. But make it our oven-fried way, and your guy won't be singing "the blues" because his trousers are too tight.

4   (4-ounce) skinned and boned
        chicken breast halves
½   cup all-purpose flour
¼   teaspoon salt
¼   teaspoon pepper
½   cup egg substitute
1   cup crushed corn flakes cereal
        (see facing page)

1   tablespoon chopped fresh parsley
1   teaspoon dried tarragon
4   (1-ounce) slices nonfat Swiss cheese
4   slices lean Canadian bacon
        or lean ham
    Vegetable cooking spray

Place chicken between 2 sheets of heavy-duty plastic wrap, and flatten to ¼-inch thickness using a meat mallet or rolling pin.

Combine flour, salt, and pepper in shallow dish. Place egg substitute in a bowl. Combine corn flake crumbs, parsley, and tarragon in a shallow dish.

Top each breast half with a slice of cheese and Canadian bacon; roll up. While holding roll together, dredge in flour mixture, dip in egg substitute, and dredge in corn flake crumb mixture. Set chicken, seam side down, on a baking sheet coated with cooking spray. Spray chicken lightly with cooking spray. Bake, uncovered, at 350° for 30 minutes, turning after 15 minutes. Yield: 4 servings.

Things
MOTHER NEVER TOLD YOU

Instead of using store-bought corn flake crumbs for coating fish or chicken, crush your own crumbs from corn flakes cereal. You'll get slightly bigger crumbs and a crispier texture. Pour corn flakes cereal into a heavy-duty, zip-top plastic bag, and crush with a rolling pin. One 10-ounce box of corn flakes cereal yields about $2^1/_2$ cups of crumbs. Freeze any leftover crumbs.

Stuff the Chicken, Not Your Man
Baked Chicken with Cornbread Stuffing

This comfort food will make your man feel pampered. We recommend serving this dish with our Waist-Away Mashed Potatoes (see page 72).

1 (3- to 4-pound) broiler-fryer	1 (14½-ounce) can ready-to-serve
Salt	chicken broth, divided
Pepper	1 (8-ounce) package cornbread stuffing
½ pound fresh mushrooms, sliced	1 (8-ounce) can sliced water
¾ cup diced celery	chestnuts, drained
¼ cup chopped onion	2 teaspoons rubbed sage

Sprinkle cavity of chicken with salt and pepper. Cook mushrooms, celery, and onion in ½ cup chicken broth in a nonstick skillet over medium heat until tender. Combine cornbread stuffing and water chestnuts in a large bowl; add mushroom mixture and sage. Gradually stir in remaining broth. Stuff cornbread mixture into cavity of chicken. Close cavity, and secure with wooden picks; truss. Bake, uncovered, at 350° for 1 hour and 30 minutes or until meat thermometer inserted in meaty part of thigh registers 180°. Remove skin before serving. Yield: 6 servings.

Finger-Licking Fantasy
Oven-Fried Chicken

You may believe that when you fry chicken, the oil remains in the skillet. Sorry, but that isn't the case. Two pieces of fried chicken weigh in at 729 calories and 46 grams of fat. We've developed a method for oven-frying chicken that turns out extra-crispy on the outside, yet moist and tender inside. Southern gentlemen cock-a-doodle-do for this.

1   cup egg substitute
1   cup all-purpose flour
1   teaspoon ground red pepper
¼   teaspoon salt
¼   teaspoon black pepper
¼   teaspoon Old Bay seasoning

1½   cups crushed corn flakes cereal
         (see page 49)
1   (2-pound) broiler-fryer, cut up
         and skinned
     Vegetable cooking spray

Place egg substitute in a shallow dish. Combine flour and next 4 ingredients in a shallow dish. Place corn flake crumbs in a shallow dish. Dredge chicken in flour mixture, dip in egg substitute, and dredge in crumbs, coating well. Place on a baking sheet coated with cooking spray. Spray chicken with cooking spray. Chill at least 1 hour. Bake, uncovered, at 400° for 1 hour or until crisp and golden. Yield: 4 servings.

He'll Be Your Hot Dish

Pheasant and Broccoli Hot Dish

This dish is dedicated to our Dad and his dog Barney for risking life and limb hunting pheasant for our dinners. You can find pheasant at your local specialty market, or you can substitute chicken. This warm and satisfying dish will surely make your Hot Dish want to satisfy you!

4   skinned pheasant breast halves
      or 4 skinned chicken breast halves
2   (14½-ounce) cans ready-to-serve
      chicken broth
      Vegetable cooking spray
1   pound fresh broccoli, chopped
      (about 5 cups)
2   (16-ounce) cans reduced-fat cream
      of chicken soup

½   cup nonfat mayonnaise
1   cup (4 ounces) shredded reduced-fat
      Cheddar cheese, divided
1   tablespoon lemon juice
¼   teaspoon salt
¼   teaspoon pepper
½   cup fine, dry breadcrumbs

Place pheasant in a 13- x 9- x 2-inch baking dish; add broth. Cover and bake at 300° for 2 hours. Bone and coarsely chop meat. Discard broth.

Coat a 2-quart casserole with cooking spray; place pheasant and broccoli in casserole. Combine soup, mayonnaise, ½ cup cheese, lemon juice, salt, and pepper; stir well. Pour over mixture in casserole, and stir to blend. Cover and bake at 350° for 45 minutes. Remove from oven. Top with remaining ½ cup cheese and breadcrumbs. Spray breadcrumbs with cooking spray. Broil 5½ inches from heat 3 minutes or until cheese melts and breadcrumbs are lightly browned. Yield: 4 servings.

He'll Gobble You Up
Turkey Reuben Bake

When you and your man are in the mood for a no-fuss meal, gobble up this sandwich-inspired casserole. Our easy one-dish version of the Reuben talks turkey, with less than 30% of calories from fat.

3 large baking potatoes, peeled and cut into 1-inch cubes
½ cup nonfat sour cream
⅓ cup skim milk
¼ teaspoon salt
½ teaspoon pepper
Vegetable cooking spray
½ medium cabbage, thinly sliced (about 4 cups)

1½ teaspoons caraway seeds
⅓ cup nonfat Thousand Island salad dressing
1 cup chopped cooked turkey
1½ cups (6 ounces) shredded reduced-fat Swiss cheese, divided
Paprika

Cook potatoes in boiling water to cover 15 minutes or until very tender. Drain; place in a large bowl. Add sour cream, milk, salt, and pepper; beat at medium speed of an electric mixer until smooth. Set aside.

Coat a large skillet with cooking spray; place over medium heat until hot. Add cabbage and caraway seeds, and cook, stirring constantly, 5 minutes or until cabbage is wilted. Stir in salad dressing.

Spread half of potato mixture in an 11- x 7- x 1½-inch baking dish coated with cooking spray. Top with cabbage mixture, turkey, and 1 cup cheese. Spread remaining potato mixture over cheese; top with remaining ½ cup cheese. Sprinkle with paprika. Bake, uncovered, at 350° for 40 minutes. Let stand 5 minutes before serving. Yield: 6 servings.

Just Like Mom Used to Make
Chunky Turkey and Celery Casserole

If your main man hits the gym rather than driving through a fast food restaurant, make this casserole to show him your appreciation for his beautiful body. Then cuddle up to his buns of steel to encourage his fitness efforts.

2½ cups chopped cooked turkey
2 cups diced celery (about 4 stalks)
⅔ cup nonfat mayonnaise-type salad dressing
2½ tablespoons finely chopped onion
2 tablespoons Bon Appetit seasoning
2 tablespoons (½ ounce) shredded reduced-fat Cheddar cheese

2 tablespoons lemon juice
¼ cup sliced almonds, toasted
  Vegetable cooking spray
¼ cup Italian-seasoned breadcrumbs (see facing page)

Combine first 7 ingredients in a large bowl; stir well. Gently stir in almonds. Spoon mixture into a 1½-quart casserole coated with cooking spray. Sprinkle with breadcrumbs; spray breadcrumbs with cooking spray. Bake, uncovered, at 350° for 35 minutes or until lightly browned. Yield: 4 servings.

Things

MOTHER NEVER TOLD YOU

*It's easy to whip up your own Italian-seasoned breadcrumbs,
and they'll be lower in sodium than those you buy. Simply
place pieces of day-old French or Italian bread in a food
processor, and process to desired consistency. Then sprinkle
the crumbs with dried Italian seasoning to taste.
You can even freeze the homemade crumbs in an airtight
container so you'll have them ready and waiting.*

Love Bait
Oven-Fried Fish

If you're lucky enough to know a man who likes to fish, reel him in. Ask him to catch you a walleye, a delicious white fish found in the Northern part of the country. If the walleye aren't biting or aren't available where you live, you can substitute any other firm white fish. Have your next fish-fry our way, and you may get a few nibbles!

½ cup nonfat mayonnaise
¼ cup finely chopped onion
¼ cup finely chopped sweet pickles
¼ teaspoon lemon juice
⅛ teaspoon paprika
   Dash of hot sauce
1 pound walleye or other firm white fish fillets, cut into 1-ounce pieces
1 cup all-purpose flour

¼ teaspoon salt
¼ teaspoon black pepper
¼ teaspoon ground red pepper
1 cup egg substitute
2 cups crushed corn flakes cereal (see page 49)
½ cup grated Romano or Asiago cheese
   Vegetable cooking spray

Combine first 6 ingredients in a small bowl, and stir well. Cover sauce, and chill thoroughly.

Pat fish dry with paper towels. Combine flour, salt, black pepper, and red pepper in a shallow dish; set aside. Place egg substitute in a bowl; set aside. Combine corn flake crumbs and cheese in a shallow dish. Dredge each piece of fish in flour mixture; dip in egg substitute, and dredge in corn flake crumbs mixture, coating well. Set fish on a baking sheet coated with cooking spray. Chill 1 hour. Spray fish with cooking spray. Bake, uncovered, at 350° for 15 minutes; turn and bake 15 additional minutes or until browned and crispy. Serve with chilled sauce. Yield: 4 servings.

Sex and the Sea
Sea Scallops

This elegant sea scallop entrée is sure to win you brownie points…you can collect later in the evening.

Vegetable cooking spray
¾ pound fresh mushrooms, sliced
1½ tablespoons minced shallots
2 tablespoons all-purpose flour
⅔ cup evaporated skimmed milk
⅔ cup dry vermouth or dry white wine

1 tablespoon lemon juice
1 bay leaf
½ teaspoon salt
1½ pounds sea scallops (see facing page)
⅓ cup fine, dry breadcrumbs
¼ cup grated Parmesan cheese
1 tablespoon dried parsley flakes

Coat a large nonstick skillet with cooking spray; place over medium heat until hot. Add mushrooms and shallot, and cook, stirring constantly, until vegetables are tender. (Add 2 tablespoons water to prevent sticking, if necessary.) Set aside.

Place flour in a bowl; gradually add skimmed milk, stirring with a wire whisk until blended. Pour milk mixture into a large nonstick skillet. Add vermouth, lemon juice, bay leaf, and salt; bring to a boil. Reduce heat, and cook, stirring constantly, 3 minutes or until thickened. Add mushroom mixture and scallops; cook 4 minutes or until scallops are opaque. Remove and discard bay leaf. Remove from heat.

Spoon mixture evenly into individual oven-proof serving dishes. Combine breadcrumbs, cheese, and parsley; sprinkle evenly over scallop mixture. Spray with cooking spray. Broil 5½ inches from heat 1 minute or until golden. Yield: 2 servings.

Things
MOTHER NEVER TOLD YOU

*All scallops are not created equal. There are bay
scallops and sea scallops. Bay scallops are very tiny
(about ¹/₂ inch in diameter) and their meat is on the sweet
side. Sea scallops average 1¹/₂ inches in diameter and are
slightly chewier. All fresh scallops should have
a sweet smell and a moist sheen.*

The Horizontal Hula
Pineapple and Canadian Bacon Pizza

You'll have to look long and hard to find a man who doesn't like a good pizza. But one slice of pizza with the works packs 400 calories and 23 grams of fat. This light pineapple-topped version will have him going back for seconds, but that's OK. You'll still be able to get him into a swimsuit.

¾ cup water
1 (6-ounce) can tomato paste
1½ teaspoons dried oregano
1 teaspoon dried basil
½ to 1 teaspoon dried crushed red
    pepper
1 (10-ounce) thin Boboli pizza crust

8 slices lean Canadian bacon
1 (15¼-ounce) can pineapple chunks,
    drained
½ cup (2 ounces) shredded reduced-fat
    mozzarella cheese
¼ cup grated Romano cheese

Combine first 5 ingredients in a small saucepan; cook, uncovered, over medium heat 10 minutes, stirring occasionally. Spread sauce over crust. Top with Canadian bacon and pineapple. Sprinkle with cheeses. Place pizza on a baking sheet. Bake at 450° for 8 to 10 minutes or until lightly browned. Yield: 2 servings.

He Won't Clam Up
Roasted Garlic and Clam Pizza

Occasionally, even the best of couples can experience a breakdown in communication. We created this recipe when mad at our men, thinking they'd hate it. Much to our dismay, they loved it and now crave it weekly. Don't hesitate about the roasted garlic and clam combo. The roasted garlic has a sweet, mellow flavor we think you'll both enjoy.

¾ cup water
1 (6-ounce) can tomato paste
1½ teaspoons dried oregano
1 teaspoon dried basil
½ to 1 teaspoon dried crushed red pepper
1 (10-ounce) thin Boboli pizza crust

2 (6½-ounce) cans minced clams, rinsed and drained
1 head garlic, roasted and chopped (see page 13)
½ cup (2 ounces) shredded reduced-fat mozzarella cheese
¼ cup grated Romano cheese

Combine first 5 ingredients in a small saucepan; cook, uncovered, over medium heat 10 minutes. Spread sauce over crust. Top with clams and garlic. Sprinkle with cheeses. Place pizza on a baking sheet. Bake at 450° for 8 to 10 minutes or until lightly browned. Yield: 2 servings.

Under the Covers
Ricotta- and Spinach-Stuffed Ravioli

Set the pasta maker on the counter so your man will think you've slaved all day in the kitchen. Then go buy something sexy to wear at dinner. You'll have plenty of time to shop—this quick-and-easy ravioli is made from wonton wrappers!

¾ cup nonfat ricotta cheese
¼ cup frozen chopped spinach, thawed and drained
2 tablespoons grated Parmesan cheese
1½ tablespoons chopped raisins
1½ tablespoons pine nuts or chopped almonds, toasted

1 (1-pound) package wonton wrappers
Tomato Sauce
¼ cup (1 ounce) reduced-fat mozzarella cheese

Combine first 5 ingredients; stir well. Spoon spinach mixture evenly onto half of wonton wrappers. (Keep a damp cloth over remaining wonton wrappers while you work to prevent them from drying out.) Brush the edges of each filled wrapper with water. Place a second wrapper over filling, pressing to seal edges. Place a drinking glass over filled wontons, and cut to form ravioli. Cover and chill until ready to cook.

Bring water to a boil in a stockpot. Drop ravioli into water, a few at a time, using a slotted spoon; boil 4 minutes. Remove with slotted spoon.

To serve, place ravioli on a serving platter. Spoon Tomato Sauce over ravioli, and sprinkle with mozzarella cheese. Yield: 4 servings.

Tomato Sauce

1	(28-ounce) can whole tomatoes, undrained and chopped	1	tablespoon balsamic vinegar
		1	teaspoon dried thyme
8	Roma tomatoes, peeled and seeded	¼	teaspoon dried crushed red pepper
¼	cup dry red wine	2	cloves garlic, minced
1	tablespoon dried basil	1	bay leaf
1	tablespoon dried oregano	¼	cup grated Parmesan cheese

Combine all ingredients except cheese in a stockpot; bring to a boil. Reduce heat, and simmer, uncovered, 1 hour. Remove and discard bay leaf. Stir in cheese just before serving. Yield: 4 cups.

Use Your Noodle
Fettuccine with Creamy Mushroom Sauce

Most men think that Fettuccine Alfredo is a healthy entrée. Little do they know that the average order contains 97 grams of fat. If your little Luigi likes pasta, lure him with this scrumptious version. His waistline will thank you.

1 pound fresh mushrooms, sliced
2 cloves garlic, minced
1 cup water
1 (10¾-ounce) can reduced-fat, reduced-sodium cream of mushroom soup

¼ cup nonfat sour cream
¼ cup skim milk
¼ cup grated Parmesan or Romano cheese
1 (12-ounce) package fettuccine

Cook mushrooms and garlic in water in a nonstick skillet over medium heat until tender; drain.

Combine soup, sour cream, and milk in a saucepan; cook over low heat until blended, stirring often. Add mushroom mixture and cheese, and cook until heated.

Meanwhile, cook fettuccine according to package direction, omitting salt and oil; drain. Toss pasta with sauce. Serve immediately. Yield: 4 servings.

Enhancers

Side Dishes

Make-Him-Ogle Kugel
Apricot-Sour Cream Kugel

Kugel is a Jewish dish traditionally made with cream cheese and sour cream. Oy vay! We've replaced both high-fat items with their lower-fat counterparts for spine-tingling results. Stay away from the nonfat products for this recipe; they don't bake as well.

7	ounces wide, yolk-free noodles		2	tablespoons sugar
	Vegetable cooking spray		¼	teaspoon salt
1	cup egg substitute		½	teaspoon vanilla extract
1	cup apricot nectar		10	dried apricots, chopped
½	cup low-fat sour cream		¼	cup crushed corn flakes cereal
3	tablespoons Neufchâtel cheese, softened			(see page 49)
3	tablespoons skim milk		1	tablespoon sugar
			½	teaspoon ground cinnamon

Cook yolk-free noodles according to package directions, omitting salt and oil; drain well. Place noodles in a 13- x 9- x 2-inch baking dish coated with cooking spray, and set aside.

Beat egg substitute in a medium mixing bowl at high speed of an electric mixer 1 minute. Add apricot nectar and next 6 ingredients; beat until smooth. Fold in chopped apricot. Pour mixture over noodles, and stir gently.

Combine corn flake crumbs, 1 tablespoon sugar, and cinnamon; sprinkle evenly over noodle mixture. Spray crumb mixture with cooking spray. Bake, uncovered, at 350° for 1 hour. Let stand 10 minutes before serving. Serve warm, or cover and chill 1 hour. Yield: 8 servings.

Nibble These Ears
Creamed Corn

Americans tend to gain weight during their thirties. We say stop that middle-age spread before it starts! This creamy corn dish is a good beginning.

Vegetable cooking spray
½ cup sliced green onions
2¼ cups evaporated skimmed milk
1 tablespoon sugar
½ teaspoon salt
½ teaspoon ground red pepper
⅓ cup all-purpose flour
1 cup egg substitute
3½ cups canned whole kernel corn, drained

Coat a large nonstick skillet with cooking spray; place over medium heat until hot. Add green onions, and cook, stirring constantly, 1 minute. Stir in milk and next 3 ingredients; simmer 4 minutes (do not boil). Remove from heat, and set aside.

Combine flour and egg substitute in a large mixing bowl. Beat at medium speed of an electric mixer 1 minute or until blended. Gradually add green onion mixture, stirring until blended. Stir in corn. Pour into an 11- x 7- 1½-inch baking dish coated with cooking spray. Bake, uncovered, at 350° for 1 hour or until a knife inserted near center comes out clean. Serve immediately. Yield: 6 servings.

Savage Cabbage
Sweet-and-Sour Cabbage

Nutritional guidelines suggest that we eat five servings of fruits and vegetables a day. This tangy side dish is virtually fat free, so it's a great way to increase your man's vegetable intake without kissing his healthy weight good-bye.

6	whole cloves	2	large apples, peeled, cored, and diced
6	black peppercorns	1	onion, thinly sliced
2	whole allspice	1½	cups water
1	bay leaf	1	cup cider vinegar
1	medium-size red cabbage, thinly sliced	½	cup sugar
		½	teaspoon salt

Tie first 4 ingredients in a cheesecloth bag. Place spice bag, cabbage, and remaining ingredients in a stockpot; bring to a boil. Cover, reduce heat, and simmer 1½ hours. Remove and discard spice bag before serving. Yield: 6 servings.

Waist-Away Mashed Potatoes
Garlic Mashed Potatoes

Men love mashed potatoes. And your spud stud will savor our secret low-fat dish, made with garlic and nonfat sour cream instead of butter and cream. Just set out a butter dish, and let him think it's Mom's recipe lavished in the yellow sin.

6	medium baking potatoes, peeled and quartered	½	teaspoon salt
1	cup evaporated skimmed milk	¼	teaspoon pepper
½	cup nonfat sour cream	2	heads garlic, roasted (see page 13)
			Vegetable cooking spray

Cook potatoes in boiling water to cover 20 minutes or until tender. Drain; place in a mixing bowl. Add milk, sour cream, salt, and pepper; beat at medium speed of electric mixer until smooth. Stir in garlic pulp. Spoon mixture into an 11- x 7- x 1½-inch baking dish coated with cooking spray. Cover and bake at 350° for 30 minutes. Yield: 6 servings.

Do-the-Hustle Potatoes
Scalloped Potatoes

Potatoes are one of America's favorite vegetables. They're also high in carbohydrates, an important energy source for dancing after dinner.

1¼ cups evaporated skimmed milk
1 clove garlic, minced
2½ pounds red potatoes, peeled and
    thinly sliced

Vegetable cooking spray
1 cup (4 ounces) shredded reduced-fat
    Swiss cheese, divided

Bring milk to a boil in a saucepan. Add garlic; reduce heat, and simmer 1 minute. Remove from heat.

Arrange half of potato slices in a 13- x 9- x 2-inch baking dish coated with cooking spray. Sprinkle with half of cheese; top with half of milk mixture. Repeat layers. Bake, uncovered, at 425° for 25 minutes or until golden. Yield: 6 servings.

You Devil, You!
Deviled Spinach

Go ahead—bring out the devil in him. After all, making whoopee burns calories.

½ cup evaporated skimmed milk
1 tablespoon cornstarch
   Vegetable cooking spray
¼ cup chopped onion
1 clove garlic, minced
2 (10-ounce) packages frozen chopped
      spinach, thawed and drained
4 hard-cooked egg whites, chopped
1 hard-cooked egg yolk, chopped

1 cup cubed reduced-fat loaf process
      cheese spread
1 teaspoon dry mustard
½ teaspoon ground red pepper
½ teaspoon ground celery seeds
   Dash of Worcestershire sauce
¼ cup crushed corn flakes cereal
      (see page 49)
   Paprika

Combine milk and cornstarch; stir until smooth. Coat a skillet with cooking spray; place over medium heat until hot. Add onion and garlic; cook, stirring constantly, 5 minutes. Stir in cornstarch mixture. Bring to a boil; boil 1 minute. Stir in spinach and next 7 ingredients. Spoon into a 1-quart casserole coated with cooking spray. Sprinkle with crumbs and paprika. Bake at 375° for 30 minutes. Yield: 6 servings.

Early Riser

Breakfasts

Yours Forever Frittata
Mushroom-Tarragon Frittata

Frittatas are naturals for breakfast or brunch. But get those creative juices flowing! Serve your sweetie a romantic dinner in bed with this hearty, yet heart-healthy, dish and a nice bottle of Pinot Grigio.

Vegetable cooking spray
½ pound fresh mushrooms, sliced
2 cups egg substitute
2 tablespoons all-purpose flour
3 tablespoons skim milk

½ cup (2 ounces) shredded reduced-fat Cheddar cheese
2 tablespoons grated Parmesan cheese
2 teaspoons dried tarragon

Coat a large nonstick skillet with cooking spray; place over medium heat until hot. Add mushrooms, and cook, stirring constantly, until tender. (Add 2 tablespoons water to prevent sticking, if necessary.) Remove from heat, and set aside.

Beat egg substitute in a large mixing bowl 2 minutes at high speed of an electric mixer. Combine flour and milk, stirring until blended. Add flour mixture to egg substitute; beat 2 additional minutes. Gently stir in mushrooms, cheeses, and tarragon. Spoon mixture into a deep 2-quart casserole coated with vegetable cooking spray.

Bake, uncovered, at 375° for 40 minutes or until set and lightly browned. Let stand 10 minutes before serving. Yield: 4 servings.

Things
MOTHER NEVER TOLD YOU

The traditional method of sautéing is to use a small amount of oil in a skillet. We eliminate the fat and still get good results by spraying a nonstick skillet with vegetable cooking spray. If the quantity of ingredients to be sautéed is large, you may want to add a few tablespoons of water or broth to prevent sticking, and then drain, if necessary.

Bon Jour, Mon Ami!
Stuffed French Toast

Nothing's more enjoyable than having breakfast together (well, almost nothing). Make it extra-special by surprising your man with this fruit-stuffed French toast. He may be grateful enough to finally get to your "honey-do" list.

4 diagonally cut, 1-inch-thick slices French bread (see facing page)
½ cup nonfat ricotta cheese
3 tablespoons finely chopped golden raisins
2 tablespoons shredded reduced-fat mozzarella cheese
1 teaspoon sugar
¼ teaspoon vanilla
½ cup skim milk
½ cup egg substitute
Vegetable cooking spray
1 (16-ounce) can apricot halves in juice, undrained
1 ripe banana, sliced

Cut a horizontal slit in each slice of French bread to form a pocket. Set bread slices aside.

Combine ricotta cheese and next 4 ingredients in a small bowl; stir well. Stuff about 2 tablespoons ricotta cheese mixture into each bread pocket.

Combine milk and egg substitute in a shallow dish. Dip stuffed bread into milk mixture, turning to coat (allow enough time for mixture to soak into bread).

Coat an electric griddle with cooking spray; preheat to 350°. Cook bread 5 minutes on each side or until browned. Set aside, and keep warm.

Combine apricots (with juice) and banana in a small saucepan; cook over low heat until thoroughly heated. Serve warm over French toast. Yield: 2 servings.

MOTHER NEVER TOLD YOU

French toast works best when you use day-old bread. The drier bread soaks up more of the milk mixture and holds its texture better than fresh bread does.

Make-Him-Flip Flap Jacks
Spiced Pancakes

Breakfast is the most important meal of the day, so be sure you feed your man something nutritious. We suggest this pancake. It cuts fat without cutting flavor.

1½	cups all-purpose flour		⅛	teaspoon ground allspice
1	teaspoon baking soda		⅛	teaspoon ground nutmeg
½	teaspoon salt		1½	cups nonfat buttermilk
1	tablespoon sugar		¼	cup egg substitute
½	teaspoon ground ginger		2	tablespoons applesauce
½	teaspoon ground cinnamon			Vegetable cooking spray
¼	teaspoon ground cloves			

Combine first 9 ingredients in a medium bowl; stir well. Combine buttermilk, egg substitute, and applesauce in a large bowl; stir with a wire whisk until blended. Add dry ingredients, and stir just until blended (batter should be fairly lumpy).

Coat griddle with cooking spray; preheat to 350°. Pour about ¼ cup batter for each pancake onto hot griddle. Cook pancakes until tops are covered with bubbles and edges look cooked; turn and cook other side. Yield: 4 servings.

Get-Him-Wed Fruit Bread
Cranberry-Orange Bread

We use applesauce instead of vegetable oil in this one-bowl quick bread. It keeps the bread moist and flavorful, while cutting fat and calories. This quick and easy bread doesn't require kneading or rising, which gives you more leisure time with your loverboy.

2 cups all-purpose flour
1½ teaspoons baking powder
½ teaspoon baking soda
1 teaspoon salt
1 cup sugar
¼ cup orange juice

¼ cup egg substitute
2 tablespoons applesauce
1 cup sliced fresh cranberries or frozen cranberries, thawed and drained
1 tablespoon grated orange rind
Vegetable cooking spray

Combine first 5 ingredients in a large bowl; stir well. Add orange juice, egg substitute, and applesauce, stirring until moist. Fold in cranberries and orange rind. Pour batter into a 9- x 5- x 3-inch loafpan coated with cooking spray. Bake, uncovered, at 350° for 1 hour or until a wooden pick inserted in center comes out clean. Cool in pan on a wire rack 10 minutes; remove from pan, and cool completely on wire rack. Yield: 1 loaf.

Wedding Rice Pudding
Rice Pudding with Raisins

Brides like to impress their husbands with their cooking, so newlyweds tend to gain a little weight during their first year of marriage. This breakfast pudding will warm the groom up without expanding his tummy. It can also be served as a dessert.

2½ cups plus 2 tablespoons skim milk, divided
⅔ cup medium-grain rice, uncooked
⅓ cup sugar
1 teaspoon vanilla
½ cup raisins
1 egg yolk
½ teaspoon ground nutmeg
Additional ground nutmeg
Ground cinnamon

Combine 2½ cups milk, rice, sugar, and vanilla in a medium saucepan; bring to a boil. Cover, reduce heat, and cook 20 to 25 minutes or until liquid is absorbed and rice is tender, stirring often.

Combine remaining 2 tablespoons milk, raisins, egg yolk, and ½ teaspoon nutmeg in a small bowl; stir well. Gradually add to rice mixture, stirring constantly; cook, stirring constantly, until thickened. Sprinkle with additional ground nutmeg and cinnamon. Serve warm or chilled. Yield: 4 servings.

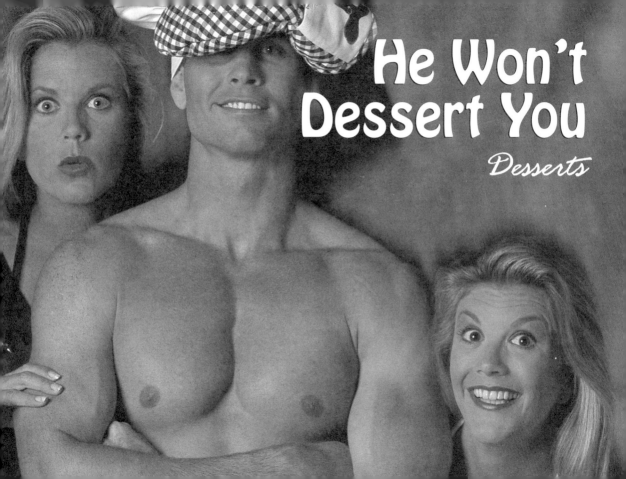

He Won't
Dessert You

Desserts

Captain "Hook Him" Cake
Rum Cake

Sure, this is a healthy cookbook, but where would desserts be without sugar? New research shows that sugar might be linked to improved memory. This finding is preliminary, but don't hesitate to do your own delicious research with your sweetie.

¼ cup chopped pecans
1 tablespoon sugar
   Vegetable cooking spray
1 (18.5-ounce) package yellow cake
      mix with pudding
1 (3.5-ounce) package vanilla instant
      pudding mix

½ cup water
1 cup dark rum, divided
½ cup applesauce
1 cup egg substitute
1 cup sugar
¼ cup butter or margarine
¼ cup water

Combine pecans and 1 tablespoon sugar; sprinkle in bottom of a 12-cup Bundt pan coated with cooking spray. Set aside.

Combine cake mix, pudding mix, ½ cup water, ½ cup rum, and applesauce in a large mixing bowl. Beat at medium speed of an electric mixer until smooth. Gradually add egg substitute, ¼ cup at a time, and beat until blended.

Pour batter into prepared pan. Bake at 325° for 1 hour or until a wooden pick inserted in center comes out clean. Cool in pan on a wire rack 1 hour (do not invert).

Combine 1 cup sugar, remaining ½ cup rum, butter, and ¼ cup water in a medium saucepan; bring to a boil over medium heat, stirring often. Boil 1 minute. Let sauce cool.

Prick surface of cake at 1-inch intervals with a wooden pick. Pour sauce evenly over cake. Let stand at least 2 hours before inverting and serving. Yield: 12 servings.

Whoopee Tart
Cranberry-Phyllo Tart

Phyllo dough is a tissue-thin pastry used in many Greek recipes. Consider another Greek tradition—daytime whoopee. Research shows that 75% of American women like sex in the evening, while 71% of Greek women prefer sex during the day.

2   cups fresh cranberries (see facing page)
¼   cup plus 2 tablespoons firmly packed brown sugar
3   tablespoons amaretto
1   (8-ounce) package Neufchâtel cheese, softened
⅓   cup firmly packed brown sugar
½   cup egg substitute
1   teaspoon vanilla
    Vegetable cooking spray
8   sheets frozen phyllo pastry, thawed

Combine first 3 ingredients in a saucepan; cook over medium heat 8 to 10 minutes or until cranberries pop and mixture thickens. Remove from heat, and set aside.

Combine cheese, ⅓ cup brown sugar, egg substitute, and vanilla in container of an electric blender or food processor. Cover and process until smooth; set aside.

Coat a 9-inch pieplate with cooking spray. Place 1 sheet of phyllo on a flat surface (keep remaining phyllo covered with a slightly damp towel). Lightly spray phyllo with cooking spray. Fold phyllo in half crosswise, and press into pieplate, allowing edges to extend over sides (phyllo sheet will not cover entire pieplate). Repeat procedure with remaining phyllo, placing folded sheets across each other in a crisscross design. Trim and crumble edges of phyllo to fit uniformly around pieplate.

Spoon cheese mixture into phyllo shell, spreading evenly. Spoon mounds of cranberry mixture over cheese mixture, and swirl with a knife to create a marbled effect. Bake at 350° for 35 minutes or until cheese mixture is set and phyllo is golden. Let cool. Store in refrigerator. Yield: 6 servings.

Things
MOTHER NEVER TOLD YOU

*If fresh cranberries aren't available, you can substitute
1 (16-ounce) can whole-berry cranberry sauce for the
cranberries and the $^1/_4$ cup plus 2 tablespoons brown
sugar. You won't have to cook the sauce. Combine it with
the amaretto, and continue with the recipe as directed.*

Sweet Feat
Cherries Jubilee

Men tend to pig out on Saturdays and Sundays, a fact which probably correlates to the scheduling of NFL and NBA games. Have this low-fat treat on hand to serve in the first half, and go for a score at half-time!

1	tablespoon sugar	½	cup currant jelly
1	tablespoon cornstarch	¼	cup brandy
1	(15-ounce) can pitted black cherries, undrained	2	cups vanilla low-fat frozen yogurt

Combine sugar and cornstarch in a saucepan; set aside. Drain cherries, reserving juice. Set cherries aside. Gradually stir cherry juice into cornstarch mixture. Cook over medium heat, stirring constantly, until mixture comes to a boil and begins to thicken. Boil 1 minute, stirring constantly. Reduce heat to low; add cherries, jelly, and brandy, stirring gently until jelly melts. Remove from heat.

To serve, spoon yogurt evenly into 4 dessert glasses. Spoon warm cherry mixture over yogurt. Serve immediately. Yield: 4 servings.

Adam and Eve's Downfall
Apple Turnovers

Is your Adam tempted by high-fat and calorie-laden sweets? He may just be able to fit into that fig leaf if you talk him into eating this apple dessert instead.

1 medium apple, peeled, cored, and finely chopped
2 tablespoons brown sugar
¼ teaspoon ground cinnamon
¼ teaspoon ground nutmeg
¼ teaspoon vanilla
8 sheets frozen phyllo pastry, thawed
  Vegetable cooking spray
1 tablespoon powdered sugar
2 cups vanilla low-fat frozen yogurt

Combine first 5 ingredients; set aside. Layer 4 sheets of phyllo, spraying each with cooking spray. (Keep remaining phyllo covered with a slightly damp towel.) Cut layered phyllo in half lengthwise to form 2 strips. Spoon one-fourth of apple mixture 1 inch from bottom of each strip. Fold 1 corner of phyllo diagonally across to opposite edge to form a triangle. Continue to fold triangle down length of strip. Spray with cooking spray. Lay triangle, seam side down, on a baking sheet. Repeat procedure with remaining phyllo and apple mixture. Bake at 400° for 15 minutes or until golden. Sprinkle with powdered sugar. Serve warm with frozen yogurt. Yield: 4 servings.

Pucker-Him-Up Pie
Key Lime Pie

Kissing before dessert is a marvelous way to keep his weight in check. Kissing three times a day for one year will burn enough calories to lose 3 pounds. Pucker up!

1 (14-ounce) can nonfat sweetened condensed milk
½ cup Key lime or lime juice
1 tablespoon grated Key lime or lime rind
1 (6-ounce) graham cracker crust
½ cup frozen reduced-calorie whipped topping, thawed
8 thin slices Key lime or lime

Combine milk and lime juice in a bowl; stir until blended. Stir in lime rind. Pour into crust. Cover and chill at least 1 hour. Top each slice with whipped topping and lime slices. Yield: 8 servings.

You're Hot, He's Not
Mood Breaker

Can the Loaf
Canned Meat Loaf

It's sad to say, but there may come a time when you need to dump your man and move on to greener pastures. Make him a meal he'll never forget before you send him packing. Be kind, and use lite processed meat. But may we recommend pairing the loaf with a bad White Zinfandel? After all, you wouldn't want him to leave hungry.

⅓ cup firmly packed brown sugar
1 teaspoon water
1 teaspoon prepared mustard
½ teaspoon white vinegar
1 (12-ounce) can lite processed meat

Vegetable cooking spray
6 whole cloves
1 (20-ounce) can pineapple chunks, drained

Combine first 4 ingredients in a small saucepan; cook over medium heat, stirring constantly, until smooth. Set glaze aside.

Place meat in an 11- x 7- x 1½-inch baking dish coated with cooking spray. Score meat with a sharp knife; insert cloves. Place pineapple on and around meat. Brush meat lightly with glaze. Bake at 375° for 20 minutes, brushing occasionally with remaining glaze. Yield: 1 serving. (Make sure you eat something beforehand!)

MOTHER NEVER TOLD YOU

Good taste in wine, like men, is a personal and complex thing. When you're trying to choose just the right one (wine, that is), consider the dish's main ingredient, seasonings, and preparation method. You can either play matchmaker and pair foods and wines that have a lot in common (for instance, a sweet food with a sweet wine), or go with the opposites attract theory and pair foods and wines that contrast (such as spicy hot foods with slightly sweet wines). Experiment and choose the combination (wine and man) that gives you the most pleasure.

Different Strokes for Different Folks
Metric Equivalents

The recipes that appear in this cookbook use the standard United States method for measuring liquid and dry or solid ingredients (teaspoons, tablespoons, and cups). The information in the following charts is provided to help cooks outside the U.S. successfully use these recipes. All equivalents are approximate.

Equivalents for
DIFFERENT TYPES OF INGREDIENTS

A standard cup measure of a dry or solid ingredient will vary in weight depending on the type of ingredient. A standard cup of liquid is the same volume for any type of liquid. Use the following chart when converting standard cup measures to grams (weight) or milliliters (volume).

Standard Cup	Fine Powder (ex. flour)	Grain (ex. rice)	Granular (ex. sugar)	Liquid Solids (ex. butter)	Liquid (ex. milk)
1	140 g	150 g	190 g	200 g	240 ml
¾	105 g	113 g	143 g	150 g	180 ml
⅔	93 g	100 g	125 g	133 g	160 ml
½	70 g	75 g	95 g	100 g	120 ml
⅓	47 g	50 g	63 g	67 g	80 ml
¼	35 g	38 g	48 g	50 g	60 ml
⅛	18 g	19 g	24 g	25 g	30 ml

Equivalents for
LIQUID INGREDIENTS BY VOLUME

¼ tsp		=	1 ml
½ tsp		=	2 ml
1 tsp		=	5 ml
3 tsp = 1 tbls	= ½ fl oz	=	15 ml
2 tbls = ⅛ cup	= 1 fl oz	=	30 ml
4 tbls = ¼ cup	= 2 fl oz	=	60 ml
5⅓ tbls = ⅓ cup	= 3 fl oz	=	80 ml
8 tbls = ½ cup	= 4 fl oz	=	120 ml
10⅔ tbls = ⅔ cup	= 5 fl oz	=	160 ml
12 tbls = ¾ cup	= 6 fl oz	=	180 ml
16 tbls = 1 cup	= 8 fl oz	=	240 ml
1 pt = 2 cups	= 16 fl oz	=	480 ml
1 qt = 4 cups	= 32 fl oz	=	960 ml
	33 fl oz	=	1000 ml = 1l

Equivalents for
COOKING/OVEN TEMPERATURES

	Fahrenheit	Celcius	Gas Mark
Freeze Water	32° F	0° C	
Room Temperature	68° F	20° C	
Boil Water	212° F	100° C	
Bake	325° F	160° C	3
	350° F	180° C	4
	375° F	190° C	5
	400° F	200° C	6
	425° F	220° C	7
	450° F	230° C	8
Broil			Grill

Equivalents for
LENGTH

(To convert inches to centimeters,
multiply the number of inches by 2.5.)

1 in		=	2.5 cm
6 in	= ½ ft	=	15 cm
12 in	= 1 ft	=	30 cm
36 in	= 3 ft = 1 yd	=	90 cm
40 in		=	100 cm = 1 m

Equivalents for
DRY INGREDIENTS BY WEIGHT

(To convert ounces to grams,
multiply the number of ounces by 30.)

1 oz	=	1/16 lb	=	30 g
4 oz	=	¼ lb	=	120 g
8 oz	=	½ lb	=	240 g
12 oz	=	¾ lb	=	360 g
16 oz	=	1 lb	=	480 g

How to Find It